T0008981

KYLE BUSCH

KENNY ABDO

Fly!
An Imprint of Abdo Zoom
abdobooks.com

abdobooks.com

Published by Abdo Zoom, a division of ABDO, P.O. Box 398166, Minneapolis, Minnesota 55439. Copyright © 2022 by Abdo Consulting Group, Inc. International copyrights reserved in all countries. No part of this book may be reproduced in any form without written permission from the publisher. Fly!™ is a trademark and logo of Abdo Zoom.

Printed in the United States of America, North Mankato, Minnesota.
102021
012022

THIS BOOK CONTAINS RECYCLED MATERIALS

Photo Credits: Alamy, AP Images, Getty Images, iStock, Shutterstock
Production Contributors: Kenny Abdo, Jennie Forsberg, Grace Hansen
Design Contributors: Candice Keimig, Neil Klinepier

Library of Congress Control Number: 2021940203

Publisher's Cataloging-in-Publication Data

Names: Abdo, Kenny, author.
Title: Kyle Busch / by Kenny Abdo
Description: Minneapolis, Minnesota : Abdo Zoom, 2022 | Series: NASCAR biographies | Includes online resources and index.
Identifiers: ISBN 9781098226831 (lib. bdg.) | ISBN 9781644946862 (pbk.) | ISBN 9781098227678 (ebook) | ISBN 9781098228095 (Read-to-Me ebook)
Subjects: LCSH: Busch, Kyle--Juvenile literature. | Automobile racing drivers-Biography--Juvenile literature. | Stock car drivers--Biography--Juvenile literature. | NASCAR (Association)--Juvenile literature. | Stock car racing--Juvenile literature.
Classification: DDC 796.72092--dc23

TABLE OF CONTENTS

KYLE BUSCH

Hitting top speeds and collecting wins, Kyle Busch has seen the checkered flag more than most!

As the youngest winner in the NASCAR **Cup Series**, Busch has earned the respect of the older, more seasoned drivers.

STANLEY

EARLY YEARS

Kyle Busch was born in Las Vegas, Nevada, in 1985.

OREGON

IDAHO

NEVADA

UTAH

CALIFORNIA

Las Vegas

ARIZONA

At just six years old, Busch built his own go-kart. He learned how to drive by racing around the family's neighborhood!

When he turned 13, Busch began his racing career. He became NASCAR's youngest **pole** winner in a **Cup Series** when he was 19.

THE BIG TIME

In 2005, Busch became the 14th of only 28 drivers to win a race in each of NASCAR's three national **series**!

In 2009, Busch became the first driver to win two of NASCAR's top races in the same day. The next year, he became the first driver to win races in all three of NASCAR's top **series** in the same weekend!

Busch won his 100th NASCAR race in 2011. He was only the third driver in NASCAR history to do so. At the end of the 2015 season, Busch won his first Sprint **Cup Series Championship.**

That same year, Busch was involved in a multi-car accident during the Xfinity **Series**. He suffered serious leg and foot injuries. After four months, Busch returned and won the Xfinity series!

Busch earned his record 102nd NASCAR Xfinity **Series** win in 2021! That same year, he joined the 23XI Racing team, owned by basketball legend Michael Jordan!

LEGACY

By 2021, Busch had 222 victories across all three NASCAR **series**. He ranks ninth on the all-time wins list. Busch is also the record-holder for the **Camping World Truck Series** wins.

Busch formed the Kyle Busch Foundation at the beginning of his career. He then started the Kyle and Samantha Busch Bundle of Joy Fund, a **charity** that helps families in need.

Though Busch has already had many career accomplishments, more victories await him at the finish line.

GLOSSARY

Camping World Truck Series – a NASCAR series where modified pickup trucks race.

championship – a game held to find a first-place winner.

charity – an organization set up to provide help and raise money for those in need.

Cup Series – the top racing series of NASCAR where 16 drivers compete for the championship. The first nine races are three rounds, with four participants cut after each.

pole – the fastest time in qualifying.

series – a set of events in order.

ONLINE RESOURCES

Booklinks
NONFICTION NETWORK
FREE! ONLINE NONFICTION RESOURCES

To learn more about Kyle Busch, please visit abdobooklinks.com or scan this QR code. These links are routinely monitored and updated to provide the most current information available.

INDEX